A buy
· guide

G000269691

Retirement Housing

A buyer's guide to
Retirement Housing

Produced by an Age Concern
England/ROOM Working Group

BOOKS

© Age Concern England and ROOM, the National Council for Housing and Planning 1995

First published July 1985
Revised 1986 and 1989
Revised 1995
Revised 2001

Published by Age Concern England
1268 London Road
London SW16 4ER

Editors Rashida Bharmal and Chris Griffin
Production Marion Peat and Vinnette Marshall
Design and typesetting GreenGate Publishing Services
Printed in Great Britain by Bell & Bain Ltd, Glasgow

A catalogue record for this book is available from the British Library.

ISBN 0-86242-339-2

Bulk orders
Age Concern England is pleased to offer customised editions of all its titles to UK companies, institutions or other organisations wishing to make a bulk purchase. For further information, please contact the Publishing Department at the address on this page. Tel: 020 8765 7200. Fax: 020 8765 7211. Email: books@ace.org.uk

Contents

Acknowledgements

The Working Group would like to express its thanks to members of previous working groups, particularly to David Bookbinder and Ray Walker, who coordinated the original guide in 1985, when they were Housing Information and Policy Officer at Age Concern England and Director of the then National Housing and Town Planning Council, respectively. Early contributors include: Jane Minter, Senior Adviser, Elderly People's Housing, Housing Associations Charitable Trust; Mike Morris, Chief Executive, Sutton Housing Trust; Vernon Tattersall, formerly Director, Hanover Housing Association; and Bill Chase, formerly Managing Director, Village Green Ltd.

This edition was completed thanks to the suggestions and guidance of the current working group and the assistance of members of the Sheltered Housing Group, Sussex Gerontology Network, especially Jeanette Blyth and Jane Trow. Other experts, including managers, builders and occupants of retirement housing, also made useful contributions and comments on the text.

Finally, we thank Evelyn Holgate and the Elderly Accommodation Counsel for checking the manuscript.

Introduction

Housing options

Retirement can bring with it a new freedom. There are numerous opportunities to do things if you are free to enjoy them and if you don't have too many other responsibilities. Living in the right sort of house in the right sort of place can help you enjoy your retirement. Living in the wrong place can bring all kinds of problems which may stop you enjoying yourself to the full.

Many more people are now reaching retirement age as home owners rather than tenants. If you own your home then you have to maintain it. Climbing up a ladder and painting the window frames is rarely fun, and the older you get the more difficult it becomes. Gardening may also have become more of a chore than a pleasure.

Getting someone else to do jobs for you can be expensive and you can't always be confident about the quality of the work. If your house is too large for just one or two people, you will probably have high fuel and other bills. Also, at some point in the future you or your partner may find getting up and down the stairs difficult, if not impossible. If the bathroom, toilet and bedroom are upstairs then that can cause real problems.

If you feel your present home is unsuitable, there are various options open to you which will still allow you to live independently:

- Stay put but have your house repaired, improved and perhaps modified so that, for example, more facilities are downstairs. You may be able to get a council grant for such modifications. Contact your local authority or Care and Repair scheme. This is worth considering if you really don't want to move. Also, your heating and insulation could be improved so that you are more comfortable and will have lower fuel bills.

- Stay put but convert the house into flats (if you can get planning permission) so that you have ground-floor accommodation. This can be complex and costly, and you would have to get used to other people living in what is currently part of your home.

- Try and get a council or housing association bungalow, ground-floor flat or sheltered dwelling to rent. Unfortunately, demand far outstrips supply and owner occupiers are normally given a very low priority.

- Move to another property that may or may not be specially designed to suit older people.

- Build a 'Granny flat' onto a house owned by your children.

- Stay with your children or other members of your family – a nice idea if you can put up with each other 24 hours a day or you all have the space to live your own lives!

This booklet is about another option – buying retirement housing.

FOR MORE INFORMATION

- For more information about housing options for older people, contact Elderly Accommodation Counsel (address on page 66).

- See Age Concern Books' *Housing Options for Older People* (details on page 70).

- For more information about repairs and improvements, see Age Concern Factsheet 13 *Older home owners: financial help with repairs and adaptations.*

RETIREMENT HOUSING

Retirement housing is often called sheltered housing and usually offers:

- self-contained accommodation, with a separate front door, bedroom, kitchen and bathroom;
- easy access to facilities such as shops, post offices, churches, clubs and public transport;
- flats or bungalows which can be reached without difficulty. That usually means fewer or no stairs, lifts to flats on the first floor or higher, wider doors and corridors, and ramps rather than outside steps;
- a scheme manager (also known as an estate manager, administrator, resident manager or warden) who will call for help in an emergency, and who can keep an unobtrusive eye on residents;
- an emergency alarm system so that if anything does go wrong, help will arrive quickly;
- internal features to help older people, for example waist- or knee-high power sockets and bathrooms which are safe and easy to use;
- high levels of insulation to improve comfort and cut heating costs;
- greater security, for example door entry systems, so that residents feel safe in their homes;
- companionship with communal facilities such as a lounge where residents can get together if they choose;
- a guest room where visitors can stay;
- release from the burden of external maintenance, gardening, external window cleaning, etc, which is carried out by the management organisation;
- a communal laundry.

There is no standard pattern for retirement housing schemes. They vary in size, range and quality of services and facilities, the amount of community activity and much else. Most consist of flats but some include bungalows and houses. Residents pay a service charge to cover the costs of providing and managing the facilities and services. The more and the better these are, the higher the initial purchase price and the service charge are likely to be.

Retirement housing is sometimes confused with an 'old people's home', in other words a residential or nursing home. It is worth emphasising that retirement housing and sheltered housing are terms used to describe many different types of housing, ranging from a small group of bungalows, specially designed for older people but with few services, to extra-care schemes (see pages 33–34). Extra-care schemes not only offer services such as maintenance, cleaning and gardening, a resident scheme manager and perhaps other staff too, but often also provide a midday meal and some personal care. It is also worth noting that retirement housing means owning a separate, self-contained home with your own front door, even though you may be living in a community atmosphere.

In some areas a fairly wide range of retirement housing may be available, so it is very important to decide whether the type of accommodation and the range of services in a particular scheme would suit you, *both now and in the future.*

The individual dwellings are usually sold on a long lease (99 years or more). A lease is necessary because it is at present the only way to set out, in a legal and binding form, the services that will be provided, the duty of the management organisation to provide those services, and the obligation of the resident to pay the necessary service charge. Because of differences in the law, most schemes in Scotland are sold freehold.

Under the Leasehold Reform, Housing and Urban Development Act (1993) leaseholders may have the right to buy the freehold of their scheme. It is possible that in future, therefore, if you buy into a scheme, the freehold may be owned either by the residents or by a third party appointed by the residents. These issues are referred to in greater detail on pages 46–49.

Retirement housing can enable you to live independently in accommodation that is easy to run. Obviously there can be no guarantee that it will always be suitable, especially if you were to become very frail. The question of becoming frail and the possibility of having to move on are discussed in detail on pages 30–34.

Because schemes now vary a great deal, you will need to look carefully at each one to see if is right for you. An increasing number of resales are becoming available, but you will still find that much of the retirement housing available for sale was built in the late 1980s. However, if you are thinking of buying into an existing scheme rather than a new one you will obviously get a better feel for the sort of community you are joining.

Finding out what retirement housing is available

Elderly Accommodation Counsel (address on page 66) maintains a nationwide database of sheltered housing schemes (for sale and to rent). They can provide information about individual schemes in specific areas including details of managing organisations involved in resales. Developers often advertise in local and national newspapers, and most will have lists of their own properties for sale in different areas. You could also check with local estate agents, who sometimes have details of retirement housing in the area, or ask them to keep a lookout for retirement properties that might interest you.

FOR MORE INFORMATION

- Age Concern Factsheet 2 *Retirement housing for sale* gives guidance about looking for retirement housing, what features to look for, and your rights and responsibilities in your home.

A different lifestyle: is retirement housing what you want?

There are many positive features of retirement housing. It allows you to continue leading an active life with the peace of mind that comes from knowing that support is available if you need it. However, there are several issues you should spend some time thinking about – and may want to discuss with your family and friends – before you begin the process of looking for and buying retirement housing. It is likely that your lifestyle will change, both in terms of your personal social life and in terms of your responsibility for the fabric of your home.

Your feelings about some of the matters discussed below will undoubtedly affect your happiness in your new home.

Ideally you should think about moving to retirement housing while you are still relatively fit and active and able to cope with the adjustments which have to be made both physically and mentally. In practice, many people move after a crisis such as bereavement or illness. Sometimes the move is arranged hurriedly by younger family members and leaves the older person feeling helpless.

PROS AND CONS OF RETIREMENT HOUSING

It is not the intention at this point to put anyone off buying a retirement home. Most residents are very happy with their choice. But from our experiences, it is clear that many of the problems or dissatisfactions people face when they move into retirement housing are based on unrealistic expectations or lack of information. This section simply raises some of the very important aspects of day-to-day living that are sometimes overlooked until after a move has been made.

Will you like living in a smaller home?

You may be thinking of moving because your present home is too large and has become unmanageable. If your retirement home is smaller than your present home, how will you feel about parting with treasured items, furniture, mementos? Will there be enough storage space? Will you and your partner feel so cooped up as to get on each other's nerves? On the other hand, will it be quicker and easier to clean? Are your fuel bills likely to be lower?

How will you feel about having someone else look after your home for you?

You may be keen to move into retirement housing because you will not have to worry about the upkeep of the building. On the other hand, accepting that a management organisation will be responsible for running the scheme also means accepting that you will not have the same control over this aspect of your life as you have in your current home. Although residents must of course be consulted over important points regarding the running of their scheme, the main management responsibility does *not* lie with them. If you think you might find this difficult to cope with, it may be that retirement housing is not for you. On the other hand, the scheme may have a residents' association in which you could play an active role. (There is more about residents' associations on page 13).

Will you enjoy having more leisure time?

A more manageable home may leave you with more time, so it is important to think about developing new interests to occupy time that might previously have been taken up by gardening or doing housework. Moving to retirement housing can give you a real opportunity, if you want it, to change your daily routine, take up new pursuits and develop your hobbies. In most schemes, however, there is relatively little scope for residents to create their own garden areas, and do-it-yourself enthusiasts should remember that the lease may prevent residents carrying out some types of alterations themselves. You may want to check whether your help in the garden or around the scheme would be welcome.

Will the new home be more convenient for you?

Most modern retirement housing includes design features to make your home economical and easy to manage. These include energy efficiency measures and economical heating systems, as well as convenient fittings and fixtures such as a shower (as well as a bath), electrical sockets at waist height, grab-rails in the bathroom or on the stairs (if there are any) and so on. Check if the new home has everything you want.

Developers also take care to try and build retirement housing in areas close to local amenities. You should check that you can get to nearby shops, public transport, medical facilities and places of worship, for example.

Will you enjoy having more company?

A move to retirement housing may mean that you have less contact with former friends and neighbours, but it also gives you the opportunity to develop new relationships. Moving into a block of flats could mean seeing more of your new neighbours than you really want to, but many purchasers look forward to this and enjoy the increased companionship and support. However, if it doesn't appeal to you then perhaps retirement housing is not a good idea.

Will you find it noisy?

Particularly in a block of flats, some people may find it hard to get used to noises caused, for example, by people using the lift or opening and closing doors. This sort of noise should not be particularly loud but it may make you realise how much you were cut off from such sounds in your former home. On the other hand, the area may be quieter than where you lived before.

Will you like the scheme manager looking in on you?

While the support of the scheme manager or warden is valued highly by many people, some might regard it as an intrusion into their privacy. You should ask yourself whether knowing that the scheme manager has a key to your home would make you feel more or less secure. This situation may be very similar to a neighbour having a key to your home now. You will know best how you react in different situations and whether you would be able to assert your right to privacy, or if you would keep quiet in order not to cause trouble.

Will there be other restrictions?

Your lease will usually oblige you to maintain the property in good order, and to restrict its use to residential purposes only. But clauses may also restrict your freedom, for example to make alterations, put up satellite TV dishes, keep pets or a guide dog and make improvements and alterations internally. Check to see if you would find any such clauses unwelcome.

What if you become more frail in the future?

Once you move into retirement housing, you are unlikely to want to move again for some time, if at all. The presence of a scheme manager and being connected to a community alarm system gives many people a greater sense of security. It can also lessen any fears you or your family may have about how you would manage if there was an emergency. You should nevertheless consider how you might feel in the future if you become frail or less able to manage on your own.

Remember If you move into retirement housing, you retain just the same rights to help from social services as anyone else. And in some ways you will be less vulnerable, because of the design of the housing and having access to people who can help you get services.

MANAGEMENT STANDARDS

People in privately purchased retirement housing have a number of legal rights under the Landlord and Tenant Acts. These rights are summarised in the Association of Retirement Housing Managers' (ARHM) Code of Practice (details on page 38). To be sure that high standards are set and maintained, the organisations representing developers and managers have looked at ways of ensuring a high standard of management. In particular they have looked at the training of scheme managers, the way service charges are calculated, how residents can be consulted on this, and the quality of the information given to prospective residents.

For schemes developed after 1 April 1990, all builders registered with the National House Building Council (NHBC) *must* comply with the NHBC Sheltered Housing Code. From 1 January 1996, private sheltered housing managers have been covered by the Code of Practice of the Association of Retirement Housing Managers. Failure to follow the Code can be used as evidence when seeking to remove a manager at a Leasehold Valuation Tribunal.

What this guide covers

The market for retirement housing has grown steadily and the choice for purchasers has widened. This guide aims to help you choose. Using it will not solve every problem, but it should help you make as informed a choice as possible, and decrease the likelihood that you will encounter any serious difficulties in the future.

Part 2 looks at the questions you should ask yourself before beginning the process of buying retirement housing. Is the social and physical environment of retirement housing what you want? The quality of life in retirement housing and your involvement both in the social activities of a scheme and in its management are considered. It looks at the location and design of retirement housing and what features and communal facilities you can expect to find. The design of these facilities and of the accommodation itself is very important – little details can be crucial and in some cases can make a great difference to how you live. The role of the scheme manager is crucial in most schemes, and this is also covered. Finally, it looks at the possibility of moving on. Most people may not need to move but some may become increasingly frail and need to look for additional personal help.

Part 3 looks at making the purchase. How do you raise the cash? Can you get a mortgage? What charges and running costs will you have to budget for? The many legal matters involved in occupying and reselling are covered in considerable detail, as is the management of retirement housing schemes.

Remember   When considering a scheme, you must never be afraid to ask the builder, the management organisation and the person who is selling the property detailed and searching questions, and you should always seek good professional advice. It is possible that not all solicitors will explain the meaning of the terms in the lease sufficiently clearly. This booklet may help.

Whatever sort of housing you are buying, if you are moving to a new area, think very carefully about whether you will be happy there, especially if you are on your own now or may be in the future. Ask yourself what you think retirement housing will provide for you. See Age Concern Books' *Housing Options for Older People* (details on page 70). The following checklist of key questions may help you decide whether moving to retirement housing would be the right choice for you. Ask questions about where you are now, as well as where you would like to be in the future.

- Do you see retirement housing as an alternative to residential or nursing home care?

- What would you expect a scheme manager to do for you? Have you checked what the scheme manager actually does and what they are trained to do?

- Would you mind the scheme manager 'looking in' on you without prior warning if he or she feels concerned for your well-being? **Note:** a scheme manager should never enter your home without prior warning except in a perceived emergency.

- Would you like living as part of a community (whether or not you choose to use communal facilities)?

- How important is privacy to you?

- Are you able to be assertive in a group? Would you be able to express your preferences to neighbours and the scheme manager?

- Do you like joining in communal activities? If social life is one of your reasons for buying retirement housing, would you be disappointed if there was not much organised activity?

- Would you want to join in decisions about the running of the scheme?

- How important to you is the location of the scheme?

- Is keeping a pet important to you, and will it continue to be so in future years?

The Quality of Life in Retirement Housing

Involvement and community activity

Before you make a decision about buying retirement housing, it is important to think not only about the legal and financial aspects of such a commitment but also about the sort of lifestyle and activities that you will enjoy, and the sort of people who will be your neighbours. You should also think about how you would feel about participating in a community, either in terms of social activities or in terms of making decisions about the management of your home and surroundings. You have the right to control the environment you live in: it is *your home*. But in retirement housing, you also have a responsibility to your neighbours to share some elements of a lifestyle you have all chosen, and to maintain both the bricks and mortar of your home and the social atmosphere of the scheme for future residents.

Most schemes have communal areas such as a lounge or dining room where residents can gather to take part in activities. This means that, whether you choose to participate or not, there is likely to be some degree of group activity going on close by your home.

However, you may be able to buy a flat that is well away from communal areas, if that is your wish.

Retirement schemes that are already established have often developed their own particular character, which can be difficult to change. So, above all, it is important that you are comfortable with the 'feel' of a scheme. You may want to meet existing residents at a coffee morning or other social gathering so that you can judge how you would 'fit in'. You might arrange to do this at the same time as you meet the scheme manager or warden.

Communal activities in a retirement scheme can range from going to coffee mornings with your neighbours to actively supporting a residents' association in decisions about the management of the scheme. Every resident should feel free to take part in any of these activities, and it should be up to you to choose to be a leader or a participant, or indeed to decide that you would rather not get involved at all.

INVOLVEMENT IN THE MANAGEMENT OF THE SCHEME

Until now, you have probably been used to making decisions about your home by yourself, with a partner or after discussion with family members. In retirement housing, you will still be in control of your own home, but your wider surroundings are likely to be managed by an agent appointed by the owner of the development. This may be a bonus for people who prefer to be free of the responsibility of external house maintenance, decoration and security. But if you want to do something new or do it differently, you will have to negotiate with the appointed agent – the management organisation – either individually or as a member of the residents' association. How do you feel about making joint decisions about your home?

RESIDENTS' ASSOCIATIONS

The level of residents' participation in the financial and management affairs of a retirement scheme can vary enormously, but nowadays residents are encouraged to form formal residents' associations. The

National House Building Council (address on page 67) Sheltered Housing Code states that management organisations should actively encourage the formation of residents' associations, as long as 51 per cent or more of the residents are members, and the association has a constitution and properly elected officials.

AIMS (Advice Information and Mediation Service for Retirement Housing – address on page 65) can give some assistance to residents who are considering forming a residents' association. The Association of Retirement Housing Managers (address on page 65) has a model constitution which is available free of charge and the Federation of Private Residents' Associations (address on page 66) supplies an information pack (price £10) which includes a model constitution.

You should ask if there is an established residents' association. What is its role in the management of the scheme? Is everyone encouraged to be involved or are there one or two dominant personalities in the association? You may find it illuminating to talk to residents who are active participants about how often they meet, how much influence their views have, what issues they are most concerned about, and what sort of relationship the association has with the management organisation.

It is likely that the residents' association will be involved mainly in decisions about domestic arrangements, such as use of the communal lounge and laundry, disposal of refuse, designation of non-smoking and pet-free areas, and arrangements for security in the scheme. Residents may also have a voice in decisions about appointing scheme staff, particularly the scheme manager. This could include discussing the scheme manager's job description, salary and daily routines, and issues such as privacy and individuals' right to choose not to have the scheme manager keeping an eye on them. Under the Landlord and Tenant Act, the residents' association must have access to the scheme's financial accounts. You should ask how such access is obtained.

SOME OTHER QUESTIONS YOU MIGHT ASK

- Are members kept informed of proposed changes in the level of service charges and the scale of management charges for services provided?
- What rights do residents have to vary the accounts?
- Are major changes to the scheme brought to the residents' association for information and/or approval?
- Are the views of the residents' association taken into account before decisions are made involving use of a sinking fund or reserves for redecoration, improvements, repairs and refurnishing of the scheme?

It is important to think about the extent to which you would want to be involved in making group decisions and how you would feel in a situation where the majority might want something different from you.

In some schemes there may be opportunities for residents to take part in other more practical ways such as running a library or information service in the scheme, or gardening.

INVOLVEMENT IN SOCIAL ACTIVITIES

There may be a considerable difference in lifestyle between a retirement scheme and what you have been used to in your previous home – in particular, an emphasis on group activities or social events. You should check what activities are organised within the scheme.

Common activities might include coffee mornings, afternoon tea, bingo, whist, bowls, exercise classes, lectures, group outings to the theatre or beauty spots, annual holidays, production of a newsletter, celebration of residents' birthdays.

Some of your neighbours may, of course, have busy lives which do not leave the time or desire to participate in scheme activities. How many residents have an active outside life? How many live almost entirely within the scheme?

Some schemes may place little emphasis on doing things together while others may have a strong feeling of community. How would you feel about spending a lot of time with your neighbours? Many people buy retirement housing specifically for the companionship this can bring, but there may be a loss of privacy or a pressure to 'join in' which some people may not welcome.

Who organises the social activities?

Is there a social committee and is this part of the residents' association or separate from it? Most scheme managers expect to organise some social activities as part of their job, but where a social committee exists, the scheme manager is likely to act as an enabler providing support for the residents. Which activities are organised by the scheme manager and which are organised by the residents? How far do the residents manage things independently of the scheme manager?

Another important question about social activities in a retirement scheme is the extent to which people who do not live there are encouraged to join in. If you invite family and friends to visit you, would they be able to take part in the group activities? How would you feel if other residents had their family and friends there? Some people are pleased to have the chance to meet new people while others find this worrying or difficult. Sometimes the communal lounge or other common areas in a scheme may be offered to community groups for meetings and other events. How would you feel about 'your' space being used in this way?

Once you become a resident in a retirement housing scheme, it is obviously your decision whether or not to get involved in the management and social life of the scheme. However, involvement in decisions about your home and surroundings, and taking part in group activities to which family and friends may also be invited as well as activities outside the home, can all add a great deal to your sense of well-being, both physically and mentally. Many residents of retirement schemes say that their move has given them a new lease of life.

Location

Where a scheme is located is every bit as important as how it is designed. Is it in an attractive area where you will feel happy to live? Can you get to the services you need? Some of the points we mention in this section may not seem entirely relevant to your present circumstances, but if in coming years you grow frailer and less active they may become more important, so they are worth thinking about now.

THE SITE

Take a close look at the location of the scheme.

- Is it pleasantly situated, sufficiently distant from any noisy or smelly factories or busy roads?
- Is the site level?
- Are there any hills to climb to get to and from the scheme to use local services such as shops?
- Does the site seem secure and private or do members of the public have access to all or part of it?

Unless you specifically want an isolated country retreat, the scheme should not be situated away from the community as a whole. There should be a range of local facilities to meet your everyday needs. You should check:

- Is the scheme in or near the centre of an established community?
- Are there shops, post offices, banks, chemists and medical services within easy and safe walking distance?
- Is the scheme within easy reach of community facilities such as parks, libraries, churches, pubs, clubs and day centres?
- Are the above facilities mainly aimed at tourists and therefore possibly seasonal or of limited value to permanent residents? Are any of them threatened with closure?

One potential problem which can affect anyone, whether you are in retirement housing or not, is that an area can change in character over time. Your solicitor will of course tell you about any existing or proposed planning applications, but no one can know exactly what developments there might be in the future.

If you move to a scheme close to land which looks as if it could be redeveloped, or if you move to an area which is being developed in other ways (for example to attract tourism), change is more likely to affect your new home.

TRANSPORT

You may currently drive a car but that might not always be the case. You should therefore check:

- Is the scheme close to bus stops or a railway station?
- How frequent are the services and where do they go?
- Are they expected to be reduced in the future?
- What are the fares like?
- Is concessionary travel provided in the area?

Communal facilities

Retirement housing schemes vary enormously in the range of facilities available for the use of residents. These may include communal gardens, residents' lounges, guest rooms, sitting out areas, conservatories, hairdressing salons, restaurants and licensed bars. Obviously the more facilities there are, the more you are likely to have to pay to buy your new home and the higher the service charge will be.

Only you will be able to judge whether your proposed home and the facilities in the scheme meet your requirements and provide the most affordable and appropriate deal for you.

Some schemes, especially those where there are mostly bungalows, may not have many or any communal facilities, and you may want to think about whether you would miss out on these. In schemes with fewer communal facilities the service charge is likely to be lower.

When looking at a scheme, there are some questions you should ask:

RESIDENTS' LOUNGE

- Who decides how it will be used?
- Is it for the exclusive use of residents?
- Does it have any facilities, such as a small kitchen for making drinks and snacks or a well-equipped kitchen for preparing meals?
- Are there other rooms for social activities?
- Are there any no-smoking areas in the lounge or elsewhere?

GUEST ROOM

- Is it always for the use of residents' guests or is it sometimes used for relief or temporary scheme managers?
- What facilities are there in the room?
- How much does it cost per night and how is it booked?
- Does the money raised go into communal funds?
- In established schemes, how heavily booked is it?

LAUNDRY

- How many washing machines are there?
- Can they be used with little or no bending over?
- Is the floor non-slip?
- Are the machines coin-operated or paid for within the service charge?
- Is the laundry used on a rota? If so, how is the rota drawn up?
- What facilities are there for drying clothes?

EXTRA FEATURES

Some properties in a retirement housing scheme may have extra facilities not available to all, such as a private garden or a garage. You should check on the availability of these facilities and how they are paid for.

Parking spaces

Most retirement housing schemes have residents' parking spaces but not always a space for each property. If parking is important to you, you should check how the spaces are allocated. They may be leased with specific properties, rented, or available on a first come, first served basis. You should also check what parking is available for visitors.

Design

The design of a scheme and of each home in it is vital, particularly if it is to remain suitable for you as you grow older and, perhaps, a little less mobile and dexterous. In this section we highlight those features in the scheme and in your potential future home which you should consider before you decide to buy.

If the property is brand new it may not be completed when you first consider buying. This means you can discuss with the builder the possibility of incorporating some changes in the plans for your home, should you consider them vital (this might involve additional costs). Clearly the builder will not be keen to make *major* changes, but some changes might make it easier for you to live there and indeed could make the difference between buying or not. You should normally be able to decide on some of the lighting, colours, materials and finishes to be used.

When you are considering buying, you may visit a show home. These are usually fitted out to a high standard by experienced designers. All the furniture in a show home will have been bought to fit neatly into the available space. You should remember that when you move you will almost certainly be taking your existing furniture, and it will not necessarily fit into a home which is likely to be smaller than the one you left. (Kitchen equipment is usually provided as part of the deal: check if it is.)

You should therefore think carefully about how your furniture and other household articles you want to keep will fit in. Take measurements and then try to plan out where your furniture will go. It is worth taking a bit of time beforehand so as to avoid problems when you move in.

The following are some points relating to the scheme and to the accommodation on offer that you should consider.

THE SCHEME

Size

If you buy into a retirement housing scheme, you will be living in your own accommodation in a complex with other retired people. You should therefore consider the general atmosphere of the scheme and how this may be affected by its size. Sizes vary – from a small complex of 10 to 30 flats or bungalows to developments with over 70, and in some cases over 200 units.

Noise

The level of noise in a scheme is something you may not notice until you move in. Check beforehand how good the sound insulation of your new home is, both for outside noise and for noise from neighbours or from nearby features in the scheme such as the residents' lounge, laundry, lift or refuse chute. You may want to visit at different times in case your first visit was at a time when things were unusually quiet.

Some developers put in television induction loops so that anyone with a hearing difficulty will not have to turn their volume up too high and inadvertently upset their neighbours. Most people who use a hearing aid can use an induction loop by switching their hearing aid to 'T'. This directly transmits the sound of the TV to their ear, without background noise.

Access

Schemes should be built to accommodate residents or visitors who have difficulty getting around or need to use wheelchairs. Outside paths should be level, without steps, and wide enough for wheelchair users; entry to the building should be level or ramped. Paths and entrances should be well lit.

If the accommodation you are considering buying is in a scheme of more than one storey, is a lift provided? If not, you may find yourself marooned in an upstairs flat if, at some stage, you cannot manage the stairs. Alternatively, if you live on the ground floor you might not be able to visit neighbours on other floors in the scheme. If there is a lift, is it big enough for a wheelchair? Does it have a seat?

If you are considering buying a two-storey house in a retirement scheme, it should be possible to live downstairs if later you find the stairs difficult or impossible to use. There should be a downstairs toilet and preferably two living rooms, one of which can then be converted into a bedroom. The stairs should have handrails on both sides to make them easier and safer to use and should be wide enough to take a stair lift.

TV aerials

In schemes consisting of flats there should be a communal television aerial. In schemes consisting of cottages or bungalows, check that there are individual TV aerials. If the scheme is managed by a housing association and there is a resident scheme manager, residents may be eligible for a concessionary TV licence (currently £5 a year). Television licences are free to people over 75. See Age Concern Factsheet 3 *Television licence concessions*.

THE ACCOMMODATION

Size and number of rooms

Room sizes will need careful consideration, especially if you are moving from a larger home and wish to bring large items of furniture with you. Consider how your furniture will look in its new surroundings.

Moving into smaller accommodation means less space for storing items, so consider the amount of storage space provided.

If there is only one bedroom, you may have less flexibility in your living arrangements. A guest room within the scheme then becomes essential for friends and relatives who come to visit.

Heating and ventilation

Your home should have a heating system which can keep the temperature at 21°C (70°F) throughout when the outside temperature is −1°C (30°F). Ask the builder or whoever is selling the accommodation whether the temperature standards set out above can be met.

If there is a communal heating system, you should ask:

- Does the heating system serve all the dwellings in the scheme?
- How are the heating charges assessed for each dwelling, and what are they likely to be?
- Are there individual controls for each home?
- What type of fuel is used?
- Are there any forms of additional heating?

Condensation, particularly on windows, could be a problem in a small, well-heated, highly insulated home which is occupied most of the day. Ask what measures have been taken to make sure that there is adequate ventilation and no problem with condensation. If there are other people already living in the scheme, ask them if they have had any problems with condensation.

Windows

Views are very important, particularly if you are likely to spend an increasing amount of time in your home. You should check:

- Do all the rooms have windows? If not, would you be happy in a kitchen or bathroom without a window?
- In what direction do the windows face, and how much sunlight will they get?

- Is there a good view from the windows, and can you see out while sitting down? (It is worth sitting on a chair to check how things look).
- Are windows easy to clean and to open and close, especially the kitchen window, which may be difficult to reach because of the sink?
- Do the windows provide trickle ventilation when they are locked?

Bathrooms and toilets

Grab-rails or secure fixings for grab-rails should be provided in order to assist with mobility. Check in particular that those on the bath are correctly positioned to help someone get in and out. The bath should be non-slip – and check that you are happy with its size. A walk-in shower is another useful feature. Bathroom, toilet and kitchen doors should open outwards to ensure ease of access if a person falls against the door.

Other features

Schemes often include other features designed with older people or people with disabilities in mind.

- Are there enough electric sockets and switches, and in the right places, for all your appliances? Are they in positions which ensure you need not bend or stretch to use them?
- Are outside lock releases fitted on any of the doors which have internal locks?
- Are the doors wide enough to allow easy access for people with walking frames or wheelchairs?
- Have lever handles been fitted rather than door knobs?
- Do the taps have lever handles for ease of use?
- Are kitchen cupboards fully accessible?
- Are there clearly labelled and displayed signs in common areas?

HOME SECURITY

- In schemes with common entrances, what arrangements are there for locking the main entrance door?

- Is there an entryphone system which will deter unwelcome visitors? If someone gets past that system, can you see visitors before you let them in your front door?
- What sort of door and window locks are fitted and how easy are they to use? This is important for all properties, but you may wish to pay special attention to security features if you are thinking of buying a home on the ground floor.
- Are smoke detectors fitted in each dwelling? (If not, you should have them fitted).
- Is the site protected with CCTV?

THE ALARM CALL SYSTEM

Almost all retirement housing schemes have an alarm system which can be operated in an emergency. Currently there are four different ways of alerting someone that help is needed:

- pulling a cord;
- pressing a button on the telephone handset;
- pressing a button on an alarm wall unit;
- pressing a button on a pendant worn around the neck or clipped round the wrist or elsewhere on the person. This activates a button on a telephone handset.

If someone has a fall and is not in reach of a pull-cord or the button on a telephone handset or wall unit, only a pendant system will enable them to call for help.

When the alarm is triggered, it will alert the scheme manager either in the office or through a personal bleeper. If the scheme manager and any other staff are off duty, or if there is no scheme manager, the alarm system may be linked to a 24-hour monitoring centre. You should always check whether this is the case. This may be run by the local council, or sometimes by a housing association or private company. Medical and other vital information on the person making the call should automatically come up on the screen in the monitoring centre when a call comes through. Appropriate help can then be called.

All modern systems allow for two-way speech, but if the person in need of help is unable to talk, then assistance will be summoned immediately. Some monitoring centres have staff who can speak other languages for people whose first language is not English.

You should check:

- Is there 24-hour cover through a monitoring system if there are no staff on duty?
- How can the alarm be triggered?
- Can the alarm be triggered by a pendant or only by a pull-cord or a button on a telephone handset or wall unit?
- How easily can each of the pull-cords or trigger buttons be reached?
- Are pull-cords easy to distinguish from those used for lighting?

You should ask to see the system working when you view the accommodation.

The role of the scheme manager

Many retirement housing schemes will have a scheme manager, often called a house manager, administrator, caretaker, warden or resident secretary. Scheme managers mostly live on site and often have a separate office.

In many new retirement schemes, you will be dealing with sales staff who will not be involved in the future management of your home. They may not be able to answer your questions about day-to-day life in the scheme and may be more concerned with showing you the design details and facilities that are available.

The scheme manager, perhaps more than anyone else, is the person who contributes most to the success or failure of a retirement scheme. Before buying into a scheme you should certainly meet the scheme manager. You should ask about his or her role in the scheme – both according to the job description laid out by the management organisation and according to the scheme manager's own interpretation of it.

Age Concern England supports the Centre for Sheltered Housing Studies' (address on page 65) Code of Practice for Wardens, which has been adopted by many management organisations. This sets out the duties of scheme managers including:

- to respect the privacy and independence of residents;
- to ensure confidentiality and equal treatment of all;
- to act with honesty and professional responsibility;
- to support residents with advice and help in contacting service providers.

The scheme manager is seen as an enabler, encouraging the residents to participate in the social life of the scheme and in its management.

Each management organisation has its own concept of the scheme manager's role. Tasks are of two types: those relating to the management of the property and those relating to the support of residents.

In managing the property, the scheme manager may be responsible for:

- engaging and supervising contractors for cleaning, gardening and window cleaning;
- arranging for day-to-day repairs to be carried out;
- compliance with health and safety and fire regulations – a legal responsibility;
- keeping a daily record of events happening at the scheme.

Other tasks include providing care and support in an emergency and responding to alarm calls. If a resident is unwell, the scheme manager can arrange for the doctor to call; he or she may contact relatives or social services where help with personal tasks is required. The scheme manager may also:

- build up a relationship with older people living in their schemes, giving residents information on availability and access to services and encouraging them to ask for additional support from statutory and voluntary organisations when appropriate;

- with residents' agreement, contribute to assessments and the monitoring of care packages;
- encourage and assist residents in setting up their own formal residents' association and social committee;

Scheme managers *do not* provide personal services like shopping, cleaning or cooking. Nor are they able to provide regular personal care such as help with dressing, washing or getting in and out of bed – care that may sometimes be required by frailer residents – although they will help in an emergency.

The scheme manager's job description will specify hours to be *on duty* and responsibilities when *off duty*, entitlements to leave, holidays, etc. You should ask about the arrangements for coping with emergencies if the scheme manager is absent from the site or on-site but off duty. The scheme manager will not be 'on call' or available 24 hours a day, so you should check what are the alternatives. The most common arrangement is an emergency alarm system which is switched through to a central monitoring centre when the scheme manager is not on duty. The *Purchaser's Information Pack*, supplied by builders to purchasers, must include information about the scheme manager's duties and working hours and any relief arrangements.

Some schemes may share a scheme manager with a number of other schemes and some may have no scheme manager at all. In schemes without a resident scheme manager you would want to be particularly confident that you could get help in an emergency. It is also important that the management organisation should be easy to contact on the telephone and that their staff should visit the scheme reasonably frequently. Where there is a non-resident scheme manager, he or she may still visit the scheme daily.

Remember Scheme managers who live in the scheme also have their own lives to lead, and when they are off duty their privacy should be respected as much as possible.

In the past the scheme manager was often described as a 'good neighbour', and in fact had little training for, or in, the job. Today, scheme managers are more professional; numerous training courses and qualifications exist, and career patterns have become established. Enquire about the qualifications held by the scheme manager and the training opportunities offered by the management organisation. The scheme manager's salary (and perhaps their heating, telephone and electricity bills) forms a substantial element in the cost of the scheme, which is reflected in the service charge. The cost of recruitment and ongoing training will be included, sometimes within the management fee.

A well-qualified scheme manager may therefore mean increased charges – you get what you pay for!

Many of the problems encountered in retirement housing arise from ambiguities or misunderstandings about the role of the scheme manager: what are they expected to do? What is their relationship with the management organisation? In the absence of a residents' association, will the scheme manager be the main link between residents and the management organisation?

The scheme manager is employed by the management organisation. If you have a complaint about the scheme manager, it is important that you are able to approach the management organisation directly, so you should ensure that you have details of who to contact and at what office. Information on consultation and a complaints procedure should be part of the *Purchaser's Information Pack*.

There are many variations in the scheme managers' roles and their relationship with the management organisation and residents. You would be well advised to explore these issues and ask questions to clarify them *before* you enter a scheme – do not wait until a problem arises.

Note When you buy retirement housing, it does not mean that you cannot receive local social services such as meals on wheels and home care. These services may be available if you need them. To find out more, contact social services yourself or ask the scheme manager.

Increasing frailty

Most people hope that once they have moved into retirement housing they will not need to move again. For some this may be so. But increased frailty can sometimes mean that you will find it difficult to manage day-to-day living without some outside help. You may then need to obtain some caring services within your existing home, or possibly need to move to accommodation that provides more personal care. You should consider what local services and facilities could be available to you should you need more support than the scheme manager is able to provide.

Especially if you are thinking of moving because of deteriorating health or a sudden change in your physical or mental condition, it is worth considering how long you are likely to be able to remain in your new home. If you are likely to need residential or nursing home care in the near future, you might be better off staying in your present home until then, and getting help at home or equipment and adaptations to help you cope with any frailty.

FOR MORE INFORMATION

■ See Age Concern Factsheet 6 *Finding help at home* and Factsheet 13 *Older home owners: financial help with repairs and adaptations*.

RESIDENTS WHO ARE MENTALLY FRAIL

In most cases, it is now considered possible to design or adapt a dwelling in a retirement scheme to accommodate most forms of physical frailty. However, mental frailty is much more difficult to cope with. It is, of course, an individual's right to enjoy his or her own lifestyle, but in a communal environment this should not override their neighbours' rights to peace and privacy.

Some leases may include a clause which enables the management organisation to take action if a resident becomes seriously disruptive. Generally, responsible organisations are reluctant to take any action under this clause. They will try instead, through the scheme manager and other agencies, to see that the resident receives any necessary care services at home or to advise them (and their family if appropriate) about possible alternative accommodation. In some cases, however, informal pressure to move may be exerted by the scheme manager and/or the management organisation because a resident 'can no longer cope with independent living'. You should check the scheme's policy towards increasing frailty.

EXTRA CARE AT HOME

A number of support services for older people are provided by local councils, health authorities, primary care trusts, NHS trusts, voluntary organisations and commercial agencies. People living in retirement housing have the same right as anyone else to apply for these services. The range of services can vary enormously between areas, as can the rules on who is eligible to receive them. The scheme manager should know what help is available locally, including:

- help with domestic tasks;
- meals on wheels, provided by social services, some voluntary organisations and commercial agencies;
- community nursing services such as chiropody and incontinence supplies;
- help with transport, shopping and other tasks such as decorating, often provided by voluntary organisations;
- equipment to help with various physical disabilities;
- intensive home care schemes (in some areas) which provide a number of personal care services.

For people who can afford to pay for extra care, there are a number of private agencies which may be able to arrange daily or longer-term nursing or other assistance. Age Concern Factsheet 6

Finding help at home has more detailed information about care and support services.

The following checklist covers some of the questions you should ask:

- Will the management organisation actively help you to stay in your home as long as possible?
- Is the scheme designed to accommodate increasing frailty?
- Is the accommodation sited on one floor, with wheelchair access? Does the bathroom have a shower as well as or instead of a bath? Is there equipment for residents who are blind or have partial sight?
- What sort of emergency care can the scheme manager and other staff give?
- Can the scheme manager and other staff provide more regular personal care if you need it?
- Can the scheme manager help to arrange services provided by outside statutory and voluntary agencies? Will he or she monitor their provision?
- Will your current GP visit your new home? Does the scheme have a medical service attached to it?
- When you first buy into the scheme, can alterations be made to the design of your home to make it easier for you to live there?
- Does your lease allow you to make changes, either now or later?
- If your needs change later on, what modifications can then be made? For instance, can a shower be installed to replace a bath? Can a kitchen or bedroom be redesigned? How will these alterations be paid for?
- Some schemes are designed with units with wheelchair access or other adaptations. Could you move to another unit in the same development which already has the design and facilities you need? This would mean selling your existing unit and buying an alternative one.

Extra-care housing

A small number of private developers and housing associations provide services and facilities for people who are not able to live totally independently. This is often known as very sheltered or extra-care housing. Usually an extra care element in a scheme means that the housing has been designed with the needs of frailer people in mind. The additional services may vary but usually include 24-hour scheme manager support, together with domestic assistance of the kind that a home care assistant might give. A dining room may also be provided which serves at least one main meal each day.

Extra care may be provided either in your own home or in a part of the scheme specially designed to cater for people with certain requirements. A move to another home in the same scheme might be more convenient for both you and your family than moving right away, but the move can sometimes be just as traumatic as if you had moved to somewhere completely new. You may see it as a signal of an irreversible deterioration in your health, for example. If there is an extra-care wing in the scheme, you should ask:

- Is there good interaction between all the scheme residents?
- Are frail residents included in social activities such as coffee mornings, bingo and outings?
- Do the more active residents support the frailer ones informally, or are the two groups isolated from each other?

How is the extra care paid for?

Finally, it is important to ask how this extra care is paid for. The cost of providing additional care within the scheme may be paid for totally or in part by *all* residents through higher service charges; care is therefore available to anyone who needs the services now or in the future. On the other hand, services may be paid for by those people who receive them. How payment for services is organised may depend on whether they are arranged by social services or the health authority or through a private agency. It is important to obtain all the relevant details, and to consider whether the services offered match your requirements and your financial circumstances.

It is always a good idea to ask about extra-care provision even if you do not think you will need it for many years to come, because ultimately this may enable you to stay in your retirement housing for much longer.

MOVING TO A RESIDENTIAL OR NURSING HOME

Some people might need to consider moving into a separate residential or nursing home. Residential homes are run by local authority social service departments, not-for-profit organisations and as commercial businesses. Commercial and not-for-profit residential care homes have to register with their local social services department, so information on homes in the area can be obtained from them. Nursing homes are run by not-for-profit organisations or as commercial businesses and have to be registered with their local health authority. Age Concern Factsheet 29 *Finding residential and nursing home accommodation* should be helpful.

Elderly Accommodation Counsel (address on page 66) can provide detailed information about residential care homes and nursing homes in all parts of the country, including homes for people with specialist needs.

Purchase and Management of Retirement Housing

The NHBC Sheltered Housing Code and Buildmark Warranty

In April 1990 a code of practice – called the Sheltered Housing Code – was introduced by the National House Building Council (NHBC – address on page 67) and applies to all retirement housing built after this date. It is compulsory for all developers registered with the NHBC to comply with the code where the scheme is registered for cover under the NHBC Buildmark scheme and the developers are selling or letting the housing themselves. The code:

- obliges the developer to provide a *Purchaser's Information Pack*;
- sets standards to ensure that purchasers are fully protected through a legally binding management agreement between the developer and the management organisation;

■ explains leaseholders' legal rights, as laid down in the Landlord and Tenant Act 1985, amended by the Landlord and Tenant Act 1987.

You should always buy a new property from a builder who is registered with the NHBC, as you will be covered by the NHBC 'Buildmark' defects warranty and by its Sheltered Housing Code.

Strictly speaking, the Sheltered Housing Code applies only to those schemes developed after 1 April 1990, but for schemes developed before then, most management organisations will implement it as far as they are able. Occasionally it is not possible to apply it fully – where, for example, the specific requirements of a lease purchased before the Code was introduced may conflict with it.

FOR MORE INFORMATION

■ The NHBC Sheltered Housing Code is available from the NHBC (address on page 67), price £2.50.

PURCHASER'S INFORMATION PACK

The NHBC Sheltered Housing Code obliges builders to supply all purchasers with an information pack when they pay their reservation fee. The pack must contain details of:

■ the names of the developer and management organisation and a statement of the relationship between them;
■ the purchaser's legal rights;
■ a detailed breakdown of services and service charges, including information about the 'sinking fund' (see pages 58–59);
■ a clear statement of the repairs and maintenance responsibilities of the management organisation and resident;
■ the scheme manager's role and the alarm system;
■ the consultation and complaints procedures;
■ resale arrangements and charges.

The organisation managing the development must also supply a pack to second and subsequent purchasers.

Note   Although the *Purchaser's Information Pack* must contain a lot of important information, the most significant document you will receive is the *lease* (or the transfer deed if you are buying freehold). It is crucial for your solicitor to explain the terms of the lease or transfer deed to you.

THE MANAGEMENT AGREEMENT

All retirement housing schemes must have a legally binding management agreement between the developer and the management organisation. This gives important rights to purchasers, as many of the standards relate to how the scheme is managed. The agreement will provide that:

- the *Purchaser's Information Pack* is kept up to date;
- details given in the *Purchaser's Information Pack* about services and charges are complied with;
- services for homes which have not yet been sold for the first time are paid for by the developer or management organisation, not by the residents;
- on resale, residents are not obliged to appoint the landlord to find a new purchaser;
- budgets and accounts are discussed at an annual meeting of all purchasers;
- a properly-constituted residents' association is recognised;
- any scheme manager is of good character, trained and supported by the management organisation.

THE ASSOCIATION OF RETIREMENT HOUSING MANAGERS (ARHM)

The ARHM (address on page 65) Code of Practice applies to member organisations that manage retirement housing schemes. It was approved by the then Secretaries of State for the Environment and Wales and came into force on 1 January 1996. Non-compliance with the Code of Practice may be used as evidence in any proceedings before a court or tribunal. Any member of the ARHM who is in breach of the Code could face disciplinary action.

THE NHBC BUILDMARK WARRANTY

In a small minority of newly-built schemes, purchasers have found a high number of building defects which have sometimes taken many months to sort out. **You should therefore give very serious consideration to having a full survey carried out before you make a commitment to buy.**

Even if you are buying new and the scheme is covered by the NHBC Buildmark warranty, the NHBC cannot guarantee that any defects will be cleared up automatically. The NHBC's undertaking is that, in the first two years of the warranty, during which virtually all but the most minor building defects are covered, it will get the builder to put the defects right provided it agrees the complaint is valid.

Another point to consider is that the two-year period during which general defects are covered will often have begun before you move in. If you move in a year or more after the NHBC has made its inspection of the scheme, and the property has been unoccupied, the two-year warranty period can be reduced to a maximum of one year from the date of completion of your purchase.

Between year three and year ten, only major structural defects are covered. The NHBC's definition of structure is quite specific. For example, neither roof tiles nor the layers of felt on a flat roof are considered to be part of the structure, and cracks in the walls have to be over a certain size before they would be accepted as evidence of a valid structural claim. The NHBC will always advise if you think you should be making a claim.

A claim which relates to the structure is likely to affect a number of – or indeed all – residents, in which case it would be appropriate for the residents' association or the management organisation to make the claim.

You should ensure, on completion of your purchase, that your solicitor gives you your NHBC Buildmark documents, as this will make things easier for you if you have to make a claim later on.

The NHBC will supply with your documents a booklet containing a number of helpful details about looking after your home.

Making the purchase

It is essential that you seek independent, professional financial and legal advice on buying retirement housing and paying the service charges. A solicitor, accountant or perhaps bank or building society should be able to provide this advice. A Citizens Advice Bureau, welfare rights advice centre or money advice centre may also be able to help. We also strongly recommend that you have a survey carried out by an independent, qualified surveyor, whether you are buying new or from an existing resident.

DIFFERENT WAYS OF BUYING

The vast majority of retirement housing is sold at full value and you get back the full value when you resell, minus a few administrative deductions. Many purchasers who have a house to sell before buying retirement housing can afford to make a straight cash purchase and still have some capital left over.

If you are having difficulty in selling your existing home, some developers may be able to offer a part-exchange deal. This may involve selling at a lower price than you had hoped for, but you have to balance this against the fact that such an arrangement may enable you to move when the whole deal could otherwise fall through.

If you are not in a position to make a straight cash purchase, or if you could just afford it but would prefer to retain part of the sale proceeds, there may be some other options available. These are discussed in the rest of this section. If you have any children or other close relatives, you may wish to discuss the options with them.

Note At times when house prices are static or falling, remember that it may be worth trying to negotiate a lower purchase price even if you are considering buying new retirement housing. Many people do this when they buy second-hand, but don't always think of it when buying into a new development.

Shared ownership

Some councils and housing associations provide schemes where you buy a share of the retirement housing and pay rent for the remainder. These schemes are normally aimed at people who cannot afford to make a full purchase. You will of course want to ensure that you can afford the rent. If your savings are no more than £16,000 (as at July 2001) and you have a low income, you should check whether you are entitled to Council Tax Benefit or Housing Benefit to help with the rent. If your capital is less than £12,000 (for people aged 60 and over) and you have a low income you should check whether you are entitled to Income Support to help with service charges.

Occasionally the housing association will agree to buy back part of your share in the property. Increasing or decreasing your share is sometimes known as 'staircasing'.

Leasehold Schemes for the Elderly (LSE)

These schemes, run by a small number of housing associations, involve you buying a 70 per cent share of the lease, the remaining share being funded by a Housing Corporation subsidy and owned by the housing association. On leaving such a scheme, you would get back 70 per cent of the property's market value at that time. These schemes are no longer being built, although resales in existing schemes will sometimes occur.

Again, these schemes are intended for people who are unable to afford a full purchase.

Loan stocks and licences

A few organisations (mainly charities) provide retirement housing on a loan stock or licence basis, whereby you make an interest-free loan to the organisation in exchange for the housing. When you leave or die, you or your estate receives back the sum you put in, without interest. You would normally expect the amount of the loan to be significantly less than what you would pay if you were buying at the full market value. There will still be the service charge and other costs to pay, and your solicitor will need to examine in detail your rights under the licence agreement. Check such schemes carefully.

Buying at a discount

Some developers may offer to sell at a percentage of the purchase price. Apart from any promotional discounts to encourage sales, buying at a discount will normally mean it is an 'equity-sharing' arrangement. For example, you pay 80 per cent of the normal purchase price, then when you sell up in the future you get back 80 per cent of the resale value.

Note   Unless it is a special scheme such as one involving loan stock or a 'life share' (see below), you should not consider any scheme where, on resale, you get back a lower percentage than you put in.

Buying a 'life share'

Buyers can sometimes have the option of purchasing retirement housing through a finance company at a percentage of the asking price. This buys the right to live in the property for life, after which the whole value of the property passes to the finance company. It may also be possible to buy a life share in, say, half the property and buy the other half outright.

The price of this life share depends mainly on your age: the older you are the less you pay. The younger you are the longer you are likely to live in the property, so the bigger the percentage of the purchase price you will pay. Men pay less than women of the same age (because of shorter average life expectancy) and single people pay less than couples.

It is very important to seek independent legal and financial advice before making a commitment, and if you have any children or other close relatives you may wish to discuss this option with them as it is likely to affect any inheritance.

Getting a loan or mortgage

Older people may find it difficult to get a traditional 25-year mortgage but may be able to get an interest-only mortgage through a building society (currently very few banks offer such loans). This may be a small 'top-up' loan, but can be as much as 50 or 60 per cent of the value of the property. The loan is not repaid until the property is sold or the owner dies, but the interest still has to be paid. In some circumstances people in receipt of Income Support – or near that level – may be eligible for help with the interest payments. For more information about Income Support contact your local Benefits Agency office or a local advice agency.

FOR MORE INFORMATION

- *Your Rights*, published annually by Age Concern Books (details on page 71), is a comprehensive guide to money benefits for older people.

THE BUYING PROCESS

Can my family buy for me?

Organisations selling retirement housing will normally allow anyone (for example a relative) to buy the dwelling on your behalf, or jointly with you. There is usually a condition restricting occupation to people above a certain age, perhaps 55, 60 or 65. Some leases restrict *ownership* similarly, but some more recent leases do allow ownership by a younger relative buying on behalf of a parent.

In some cases, complications can arise where the lease is in your relative's name, as in legal terms it would be they, not you, who had the important legal rights, for example to challenge the standard or costs of services. Age Concern Factsheet 40 *Transfer of assets* highlights some of the issues to consider.

Both you and your relative should seek legal advice, preferably from separate solicitors, before making a commitment.

Reserving a property

If you pay a reservation fee on a new property, you should check whether you would lose all or part of it if you were unable to proceed with the purchase. Sometimes the purchase price can increase after the reservation fee has been paid. Developers should either guarantee that there will not be any increase once you have made a reservation or state a date after which the price can be increased if contracts have not been exchanged.

Moving expenses

You will of course have to pay a deposit (normally 10 per cent) on exchange of contracts. You will also have to pay stamp duty, fees to estate agents, solicitors and the removal firm, plus any survey or valuation fees.

The service charge

In all retirement housing schemes there is a service charge which covers such things as maintenance, the scheme manager's salary, etc; this normally increases each year. It is essential that you find out how much it is, whether you can afford it, what it covers, how often it is reviewed, and whether there are any additional charges. Service charges are dealt with in detail on pages 50–56, but two points are worth making now:

- You should check whether the service charge has to be paid monthly, quarterly or half-yearly in advance.
- You should take great care to invest wisely any surplus capital you may have after selling your home, as this will be helpful for paying the service charge and other running costs.

Extra charges

There may be other specific charges which residents have to pay.

- In addition to the purchase price of a *new* property, there may be an additional one-off payment towards the purchase of communal fittings and equipment.

■ In many schemes there is an annual ground rent paid by all residents. This could be nominal or run into hundreds of pounds a year. In some schemes this may be linked to the Retail Price Index (RPI) and so lead to large increases. Check carefully the details of any ground rent review clauses in the lease.

■ If you want to reserve a parking space or garage there may be a charge for this.

■ You will normally have to pay a charge if you use the guest room when family or friends come to stay.

Check all these charges and ask if there are any additional payments you will be expected to make.

Running costs

You will of course have to pay Council Tax. You will also have to pay bills for water (unless this is included in the service charge), telephone, heating, electricity and gas. Check whether heating is provided centrally and paid for in the service charge (in most schemes each unit has its own heating system). Modern levels of insulation should reduce your heating bills but try and find out what these costs are likely to be – particularly in schemes which were built a few years ago.

Note You can get customer care charters and bills in Braille or on tape if necessary.

You may be entitled to a concessionary television licence if your scheme is run by a registered social landlord (see below), but the rules governing licences are complex and you should check the situation locally. Television licences are free to people over 75.

Can I get help with the running costs?

Check with the local council to see if you are entitled to any help with the Council Tax. Residents with a low income and savings of no more than £16,000 may also be entitled to help from the Benefits Agency, through Income Support, with ground rent, certain parts of the service charge and interest on mortgage repayments.

You can also check the situation with a local Citizens Advice Bureau or welfare rights advice centre.

FOR MORE INFORMATION

■ Age Concern Books' annual publication *Your Rights* (details on page 71) gives further information about welfare benefits.

RENTED RETIREMENT HOUSING

Most rented retirement housing is provided by local authorities or non-profit-making housing associations (often called social landlords). Both local authorities and social landlords set criteria describing who is eligible for their housing and which applicants have priority. All applicants are generally expected to show housing need, perhaps because of the condition of their present home or for medical or social reasons; or that they are either local or have a good reason for wanting to move into the area and that they are not able to buy rather than rent accommodation. In most parts of the country, social landlords receive applications from far more people than they can assist, so there may be long waits. One or two commercial firms now provide retirement housing to rent, usually at market rents. You will need to be confident that your means are sufficient to enable you to pay the rent (which will include a service charge) for as long as you live there. At present (2001–2002) you are not entitled to Housing Benefit help with the rent if your savings exceed £16,000.

FOR MORE INFORMATION

See Age Concern Factsheet 8 *Moving into rented housing* for further information.

Terms of ownership

Always take legal advice before buying a retirement flat or bungalow. The purchase of any kind of property is a complicated process, particularly if you are buying a lease, and expert help is required to coordinate the sale of your old home with the purchase of a new one. Your solicitor's job is to protect you and your capital asset. This guide explains some of the legal implications of buying retirement housing. Hopefully it will give you the confidence to proceed further with your purchase, but with your eyes fully open.

Most retirement housing built for sale is sold on a long lease, with a management organisation responsible for running the scheme. Some freehold retirement schemes (including all those in Scotland, where leasehold does not exist) have been completed, but the shared facilities and transferred responsibilities for repairs make freehold titles more complicated.

LEASEHOLD PROPERTIES

Leases can vary in length up to 999 years and are always sold on a diminishing term basis. This means that if you buy a 99-year leasehold flat and live there for ten years, there will be only 89 years left to sell when you leave. Eventually, as leases become shorter, they may start to decline in value, but this is likely to happen only when there are relatively few years left to run, perhaps under 40. Obviously a new lease will outlast a retired person, but generally the longer the lease the better. It is now possible, under the Leasehold Reform, Housing and Urban Development Act 1993, to extend your lease on payment of a premium.

You will find that your lease includes a number of requirements to be observed and restrictions on your use of the property, such as:

- Residents are required to pay the service charge as specified.
- Residents are obliged to maintain the property internally, including regular redecoration.
- Internal structural alterations may be made only with permission.
- The external aspect of the property must not be spoilt – for example by signs, posters, TV aerials or dishes, or structural alterations.

- Some leases do not allow subletting, or for the property to be used for anything other than residential purposes – check carefully.
- Some leases stipulate that anyone living in the property must be over retirement age. Check whether this applies to family or friends visiting or living with you and whether you are allowed to employ a live-in companion.
- Residents must not do anything that may constitute a nuisance to others (this may include rules about keeping pets, or specified types of pet – be sure to enquire about any such rules).
- Residents must do nothing that affects the insurance of the scheme as a whole.
- Residents may be evicted in certain conditions if they can no longer cope with independent living.

BUYING THE FREEHOLD

The Leasehold Reform, Housing and Urban Development Act 1993 gives some leaseholders the right to purchase the joint freehold of a development, should they wish to do so, providing certain conditions are met.

To qualify for 'enfranchisement', which means the right to purchase the joint freehold of a development, residents need to form a company and need to own 100 per cent of their property. Therefore, those living in shared ownership or LSE schemes do not qualify. Nor do people who have bought a life share or loan stock or who have bought their home at a discount (see pages 41–42). In addition, a majority of residents has to agree to enfranchise.

With enfranchisement, residents may decide to employ their own managing organisation or to take responsibility for providing the services themselves. This may appeal to some people, but the responsibility could prove to be demanding. Many prospective purchasers are attracted to retirement housing because, while offering the benefits of owner occupation, it relieves them of everyday responsibilities for the general upkeep of the development. This is usually carried out by the management organisation.

FOR MORE INFORMATION

- For more details about leaseholders' rights, contact Advice, Information and Mediation Services (AIMS – address on page 65) and the Leasehold Advisory Service (LEASE – address on page 67).

FREEHOLD PROPERTIES

Some schemes are sold as freehold properties, mostly those consisting of bungalows or cottages. Purchasers own the freehold of their home and enter into a legally binding Deed of Covenant with a management organisation which will then be responsible for running the scheme. It is important to remember that when purchasing a property freehold, residents do not have the legal rights enjoyed by leaseholders (for example, rights relating to service charges – see pages 55–56). However, the NHBC Sheltered Housing Code (see pages 35–37) applies equally to freehold schemes.

Management services

One of the important features of retirement housing is the package of services provided by the management organisation, for which you pay a service charge. Services normally include the provision of a scheme manager, insurance, external repairs and maintenance, gardening and window cleaning.

If you are buying a new property, the sales staff may spend most of their time showing you the obvious features such as kitchen and bathroom fittings. These are important, but the quality of the management services may have a much greater influence on your happiness and comfort. You will be handing over to the management organisation many of the usual home owner's responsibilities, so you and your advisers must look carefully at the services package before you buy. If you are not clear about the level or standard of services being provided, ask questions.

THE MANAGEMENT ORGANISATION

A specialist management organisation, either a housing association or private company, is usually involved in providing management services (although occasionally developers manage schemes themselves). A private management organisation may be independent or it may be a subsidiary of the builder. Your solicitor should ask for information about the terms of the agreement between the builder and the management organisation.

The *Purchaser's Information Pack* must contain the name and address of the freeholder, and the name, address and telephone number of the management organisation's head office and nearest regional office.

Once the individual properties have been sold, most builders hand over the management of retirement housing schemes to a management organisation. The management organisation is responsible for the day-to-day management of the scheme; for ensuring the agreed services are provided, charges set and collected fairly and efficiently. A management organisation can be a private company or a housing association. It is a good idea to ask what length of contract the management organisation has, to whom it is responsible and whether residents would be consulted before management changes were made.

If, on the other hand, the management organisation owns the freehold of the property, it will not be possible for the management to be changed by the residents unless, in extreme circumstances, court action is taken.

The Association of Retirement Housing Managers (ARHM) is a national organisation committed to promoting high standards of management practice among organisations that specialise in managing retirement housing. It is worth finding out whether a particular management organisation is a member. Copies of the Code of Practice are available from the Association of Retirement Housing Managers (address on page 65).

In addition to the information provided to you under the Codes of Practice, you should also check:

- Whether the management organisation has experience of managing private retirement housing?
- How many other private retirement schemes does it manage and where are they?
- Do experienced and/or qualified staff run the management services?
- Whether the management organisation has a good record of keeping the service charge costs within annual budgets?
- Have the increases in service charges exceeded or matched inflation over the last few years?
- How often do staff from the management organisation visit the scheme?
- Can you contact them directly as well as through the scheme manager?
- Are there regular meetings between residents and representatives of the management organisation?

If the scheme has been established for a few years, ask other residents what they think about the management services and whether there have been any problems.

The management organisation will make a charge for its services; this is included in the service charge.

Service charges and other costs

The information in the sales brochure (for new properties), the *Purchaser's Information Pack* and the lease should fully describe the services of the scheme. Potential purchasers should therefore be aware of:

- all the services and facilities provided by the management organisation, including the alarm call system;
- how the service charge is calculated and paid, including how the charges are split up between the dwellings;

- how much the service charge is likely to be in the current year and the date on which the charge will next be reviewed;
- the right of residents to query the service charge;
- what the 'sinking fund' covers and how it is funded.

WHAT DOES THE SERVICE CHARGE COVER?

Services normally covered by the service charge include:

- employing the scheme manager or warden, including salary, the cost of accommodation and related costs such as heating, telephone and other bills;
- providing a deputy/relief scheme manager if necessary and/or the cost of a central control alarm system;
- insurance premiums for all the buildings including fixtures and fittings, but generally excluding the contents of individual dwellings;
- communal water rates (if not separately metered);
- cleaning of external window surfaces, corridors, paths and other shared facilities;
- maintaining and tending the communal gardens;
- maintenance contracts on plant and equipment such as the lift, boilers, alarm systems and extractor fans;
- maintenance, repair and redecoration of the external structure and fabric of the buildings;
- contributions towards a sinking fund for long-term renewal of such items as roofs, windows, lifts, paths and drives;
- the management organisation's costs for providing and supervising the management of the scheme. Management fees are normally calculated as a fixed amount per dwelling per year.

Managing retirement schemes requires a more intensive management service than managing other forms of housing, because more services are offered. The proportion of the total service charge spent on management costs is often around 25 per cent, but it can be higher than this, especially in smaller schemes. Included in the fee paid to the management organisation will be some, if not all, of the following:

- ensuring delivery of the services offered;
- regular visits to the scheme;
- collection of service charges, accounting for income and expenditure;
- cost of annual auditing of accounts;
- recruitment and training of scheme managers;
- going out to tender for repairs and redecoration;
- supervision of repairs and redecoration.

HOW IS THE SERVICE CHARGE CALCULATED AND PAID?

The total costs of running the services for the year are estimated by the management organisation and divided in the proportion for each dwelling as set out in the lease. Larger dwellings may bear a bigger proportion of the service costs than smaller ones, but the proportion set out in the lease must be followed.

The *Purchaser's Information Pack* (see page 36) must include an estimate showing amounts for all the anticipated payments, fees and charges for the current year of accounting, broken down into clearly defined budget items. The estimate should state clearly for how long the figures will remain valid. It should also state the proportion attributable to each size of property. The example given of a proposed budget (see page 54) will give you an idea of the information to expect in your *Purchaser's Information Pack*. VAT may be payable on some of these charges.

This budget has been prepared after consultation with the residents. The service charge invoices for the year are based on this budget.

Since service charges are estimated by the management organisation in advance, some adjustments may need to be made once the costs are known. This means that the service charges could be revised either upwards or downwards when the accounts have been prepared. Within six months of the end of each accounting year (the time of year varies from one management organisation to another) you should be sent a statement showing what has actually been spent on services during the past 12 months. (If you do not receive a statement automatically, you can request one).

ANNUAL REVIEW OF THE SERVICE CHARGE

The Association of Retirement Housing Managers' (ARHM) Code of Practice states that the management organisation will provide all purchasers with a copy of the scheme accounts, independently audited, within six months of the end of each accounting period. If the total spent during the year amounts to less than the amount estimated by the management organisation a year ago, you should receive a credit either in cash or through a reduction in the next year's service charge.

Conversely, if more has been spent than was budgeted, you will have to pay extra, either as a one-off payment or spread over the next year's service charge. Experienced management organisations will try to avoid major fluctuations in charges from year to year through prudent management and realistic budgeting.

Before each review of the service charge, management organisations should consult residents and take into account all comments they make, as outlined in the ARHM Code of Practice.

HOW MUCH IS THE SERVICE CHARGE LIKELY TO BE?

The service charge depends very much upon the level of services and facilities provided; many are in the range of £25–£35 per week at 2001 prices (but service charges may be proportionately higher in a smaller scheme). The service charge does not include your personal costs such as Council Tax, contents insurance, electricity, gas central heating, telephone and internal decorating. But it may cover some of the items you normally pay for in your own home, such as buildings insurance, external repairs and maintenance, gardening and water rates.

By and large, you get what you pay for. The greater the range of services, the higher the service charge. But the lowest quoted service charge is not necessarily the best. You will need to compare

Proposed budget for the year ending 31 August 2001

		£
Scheme manager	Salary	13,000
	Relief costs	3,000
	Central monitoring	4,000
	Monitoring telephone	**500**
		20,500
Communal	Insurance	3,102
	Electricity	4,650
	Water and sewerage	3,100
	Window cleaning	2,200
	Gardening	2,300
	Cleaning and materials	350
		15,702
Maintenance and repairs	Lift	2,264
	Fire equipment	837
	Lighting equipment	290
	Door entry and scheme manager call	2,045
	Laundry	200
	Windows and fans	290
	General	1,730
		7,656
General expenses	Redecoration fund	3,139
	Contingency (sinking) fund	920
	Telephone	650
	Sundries	200
	Management fees	7,857
	Audit fees	440
	Bank charges	100
		13,306
Less: Sundry income	(eg guest room income)	950
		56,214
Lease fraction 2/82	£1,371.07 pa	**£26.36 pw**
Lease fraction 3/82	£2,056.59 pa	**£39.54 pw**

carefully the services provided for the prices quoted in different schemes.

Although management organisations will endeavour to keep increases in service charges to a minimum, you are unlikely to get any guarantee on the level of future charges, especially as some charges such as gas and electricity are outside the management organisation's control. If the scheme is not new, ask how much the annual increases have been in past years. If it is a new scheme, you could ask about any others run by the same management organisation.

YOUR RIGHTS CONCERNING SERVICE CHARGES

A service charge can be demanded only for the items which are specified in the lease. The law states that such charges should be 'reasonable' and that the works or services provided should be of a 'reasonable standard'. If leaseholders are unhappy with the cost of services, they have certain rights, as set out in the Landlord and Tenant Act 1987. They have a right to:

- obtain a summary of all the costs on which the service charge is calculated. This must contain details of all costs incurred by the landlord in the provision of the services and show how they are, or will be, charged to the leaseholders. The summary must also show details of payments made by the leaseholders already and those still outstanding, what has actually been paid by the landlord and what monies remain in the service charge account;
- inspect the accounts and receipts on which the summary is based. The accounts must be certified by a qualified accountant;
- ask the Leasehold Valuation Tribunal to fix the amount payable for services or repair work on the grounds that they have not been provided to a reasonable standard or at a reasonable cost;
- ask the Leasehold Valuation Tribunal to limit the amount of any advance payments the lease requires to what is reasonable;
- be consulted before the landlord carries out major repairs or redecoration.

Any service charges collected, including contributions towards the sinking fund, have to be held in trust. Any interest earned from the service charge account has to be credited to the account.

FOR MORE INFORMATION

■ The Advice Information and Mediation Service for Retirement Housing (AIMS) in conjunction with LEASE, the Leasehold Advisory Service, has published an information booklet giving more detailed information about your legal rights as a leaseholder, entitled *Leasehold retirement housing: your rights and remedies.*

The ARHM Code of Practice stipulates that management organisations must draw up a proposed budget each year with estimates of all charges based on whatever information is available, for example the previous year's expenditure and maintenance plans for the current year. At least once a year the management organisation must hold a meeting prior to the annual review of charges giving a reasonable opportunity for residents to comment on the proposed level of service charge. You should ask about the role of the residents' association in scrutinising and amending the accounts and proposed charges.

BUILDINGS INSURANCE

It is usual for the management organisation to be responsible for insuring the scheme, though you will normally be responsible for insuring the contents of your home. Make sure your solicitor checks that all the buildings and common areas are adequately insured and that the policy includes the cost of alternative accommodation if necessary. You have a legal right to information about the insurance policy and premiums.

RESPONSIBILITY FOR REPAIRS, MAINTENANCE AND REDECORATION

Find out, and make sure you fully understand, which items of repairs and maintenance are the management organisation's responsibility (and therefore included in the service charge) and which are yours. The division of responsibilities between the developer, management organisation and resident must be explained fully and clearly in the *Purchaser's Information Pack*. You or your solicitor should also check the lease or deed, as this is a legally binding document.

Generally, the management organisation will undertake maintenance and repair of:

- the main structure and exterior of the building, including the roof, foundations and external walls and the outside surface of windows and external doors;
- common parts of the building, including a lift if there is one;
- boundary walls and fences, drives, paths and communal landscaped areas;
- equipment, service pipes, ducts and cables within common parts of the property.

External redecoration, including redecoration of common parts of the building, is also normally the responsibility of the management organisation. Some also take responsibility for maintaining and repairing heating installations, plumbing, wiring and sanitary ware within your home. Otherwise you will be responsible for the internal repair and redecoration of your home.

It is worth asking how contributions for repairs and maintenance are calculated. Ask, too, how repairs which are reported will be recorded, monitored and dealt with. The *Purchaser's Information Pack* must set this out, as well as the system for reporting emergency repairs.

NHBC Buildmark Warranty Scheme

Under the NHBC Buildmark Warranty Scheme, the developer is obliged to remedy any major structural defect which arises in the first ten years after construction. The management organisation should normally act as the residents' agent in any claims under the Buildmark Scheme for major damage to the common areas of the building or problems which affect more than one dwelling.

Sinking fund (to pay for major repairs, renewals and improvements)

Over the life of any building, expenditure on major items of repair, improvement or renewal will be necessary. You will wish to ensure that these works are dealt with satisfactorily, as they arise, in order that the value of your home is maintained.

To prevent residents being faced with large and unexpected bills as work is undertaken, a 'sinking fund' is created to cover future major items of repair or renewal – for example to roofs, windows, lifts and driveways. Money is then drawn from that fund to pay for major building work when it proves necessary. Sinking funds may also be referred to as contingency funds, reserve funds or maintenance funds.

Contributions to the sinking fund are collected from residents; they are either included as part of the regular service charge or deferred and collected when a home is sold, or a mixture of both. The NHBC Sheltered Housing Code does not give any guidance on appropriate levels for sinking fund contributions, so it is worth finding out about levels of long-term projected expenditure and which method of collection the management organisation uses. It is also worth asking:

- How big is the scheme's sinking fund (now or intended to be in the future)?
- What will happen if the need for major expenditure arises before sufficient contributions to the sinking fund have been made?
- Will you be expected to contribute to any deficit at the end of the financial year or over a longer period?

GROUND RENT

In many schemes there is also a ground rent. This may be nominal or could be £300 or more per year. There will usually be a provision in the lease for the ground rent to be increased periodically. *You should find out how often this is.* Think very carefully before buying retirement housing with a high ground rent.

Arrangements for reselling

The *Purchaser's Information Pack* must give full details of your rights and obligations when selling your home, including any restrictions on resales, for example that you can only sell to someone over 55, 60, 65 years of age, and any charges made by the management organisation such as a fee for administering resales, and/or contributions to the sinking fund.

Ways of selling your property include going to an ordinary estate agent or having your management organisation act as an estate agent.

There are also some private agencies specialising in marketing retirement housing including:

Retirement Homes Search, Queensway House, 11 Queensway, New Milton, Hampshire BH25 5NR. Tel 0870 600 5560.

More details can be found in Age Concern Factsheet 2 *Retirement housing for sale*.

The NHBC Sheltered Housing Code and the ARHM Code of Practice state that a management organisation will not in any way impede or prevent a purchaser making independent arrangements for the resale of a property (except for LSE or shared ownership schemes developed with the aid of public funding, described on pages 40–42).

MANAGEMENT ORGANISATION INVOLVEMENT

In order to preserve the value and amenities of the scheme, however, and to protect the interests of other occupiers, and probably to comply with planning requirements, it is quite normal for the management organisation to have some involvement in the resale of retirement housing when a resident leaves. For example, there will usually be provisions in the lease, and in the original planning permission for the scheme, which restrict occupation to people above a specified age. The management organisation will want to ensure that these provisions are observed in order to maintain the scheme for older people.

In cases where resales are the responsibility of the management organisation, such as LSE or shared ownership schemes, make sure that the organisation is required to act in your best interests. You should have the right to challenge its valuation, and you should make sure that you will be repaid as soon as your home is resold. The lease should state that if the management organisation has failed to sell within a specified period (for example six months) you or your estate has the right to sell, especially as service charges will have to be paid until the sale goes through.

You should approach with great caution leases which stipulate that, while in normal circumstances you have the right to administer the sale yourself, in the event of your becoming very ill or frail the management organisation can take over that responsibility. Unless you feel satisfied about how the management organisation would decide when a resident is in this position, you may prefer to avoid signing this type of lease.

MANAGEMENT ORGANISATION CHARGES

Normally, when you or the management organisation resells, you will receive the current market value, unless you bought your home using one of the discount equity-sharing arrangements referred to earlier (see pages 40–42). There are, however, a number of deductions from the price which are normally made by the management organisation:

- any service charge or ground rent arrears which you may have accumulated;
- any contributions to the sinking fund where these are not made until resale;
- costs incurred in selling your home (these may include agents' fees).

You should examine very carefully what the sales information and lease say about this last deduction *before* buying your home in the first place. If the management organisation is acting as estate agent, it is quite acceptable for them to charge a fee similar to what any estate agent would charge.

Note You will have to go on paying the service charge until the property is sold. This applies even if you can no longer live in your home. The service charge is a liability for you, the leaseholder or your estate.

Whether or not the management organisation is acting as estate agent, they will charge an extra administrative fee to cover the costs incurred in assigning the lease, approving a new buyer, and supplying *Purchaser's Information Packs* to prospective purchasers. Even if you are finding a purchaser yourself, you will still have to pay these costs. Some management organisations make a fixed charge; others make a percentage charge, which can be between 0.25 per cent and 3 per cent of the resale price. The NHBC Sheltered Housing Code gives no guidance on the level of charges other than that they should be clearly itemised.

INHERITANCE TAX

If the value of your estate when you die (together with any gifts you make in the seven years before death) exceeds £242,000 (at April 2001), you may have to pay Inheritance Tax. If you think this might affect you, you should consult your solicitor. There are various exemptions, and making a will may help to reduce any Inheritance Tax bill. For more information about Inheritance Tax, see Age Concern Books' annual publication *Your Taxes and Savings* (details on page 70).

Note The tax-free figure and other details may be changed in the budget, so you may need to take professional advice.

Other important rights in retirement housing

SPECIAL PROVISIONS FOR TERMINATING THE LEASE

Leases for retirement housing allow the management organisation to give notice to a leaseholder who has consistently failed to pay the service charge or ground rent. Some leases allow them to give notice to a leaseholder who is causing extreme nuisance. In practice most management organisations will seek to evict a leaseholder only if, perhaps owing to increasing mental frailty, he or she is behaving very anti-socially, causing severe disruption to other residents, or becoming incapable of independent living. Even then, a number of procedures would have to be gone through.

Leaseholders have considerable rights under the law, and cannot be deprived of their home without special legal procedures being followed. It would be unusual for a court to agree to terminate a lease unless the leaseholder had wilfully ignored undertakings made in the lease and had not attempted to amend the situation.

You should be aware of any provisions relating to termination of the lease, and your solicitor will want to consider them very carefully. But remember that the intention behind them is to protect the majority of residents from someone who, perhaps because of confusion or some other mental illness, may be very disruptive and may need accommodation with a greater degree of personal support.

RESIDENTS' ASSOCIATIONS

The Association of Retirement Housing Managers' (ARHM) Code of Practice states that management organisations should encourage properly constituted and democratically run residents' associations on their estates. It also recommends that management organisations should give guidance to residents on how to set up and run an association. Residents' associations can apply to the local Rent Assessment Panel for a certificate of recognition which will generally be given if the association has a membership of 60 per cent or more of residents, a proper constitution and elected officials. The residents' association will then become a recognised Association. Of course, if you do not want to join the association you still have the right to be consulted individually on most matters.

Before you buy you should ask for details of the management organisation's policy on consultation with residents, and its attitude towards the formation of a properly constituted residents' association. Most management organisations do welcome residents' associations, but if you are not happy with their attitude, you may feel you would rather buy into a scheme with a more sympathetic management organisation.

DEALING WITH COMPLAINTS

The NHBC Sheltered Housing Code and the ARHM Code of Practice stipulate that the *Purchaser's Information Pack* must contain information about the management organisation's complaints and grievance procedure, including a timetable for action on complaints. They also make clear that residents have the right to be consulted on major issues affecting the management of the scheme. A good complaints procedure should enable individual residents who wish to make complaints in confidence to do so without difficulty.

If your scheme is managed by a registered social landlord or some private companies, you will have the right to go to the Independent Housing Ombudsman (address on page 66) should you have a serious complaint.

FOR MORE INFORMATION

■ Free leaflets and advice on how to make a complaint about social landlords registered with the Housing Corporation which are paid to manage leasehold retirement housing are available in ten different languages and on audio cassette from the Independent Housing Ombudsman (address on page 66).

ADVICE INFORMATION AND MEDIATION SERVICE FOR RETIREMENT HOUSING (AIMS)

When the NHBC Sheltered Housing Code was introduced, it was agreed that it should be supported by an independent service offering information, advice and conciliation. AIMS (address on page 65) is run in association with Age Concern England.

The service offers advice to residents who have purchased their homes; it will act as a conciliator in disputes between purchasers and managers, but it does not provide arbitration. The service aims to advise residents how best to solve any problems they might have concerning the management of their scheme. If matters cannot be resolved through the management organisation's own complaints procedure, the service can offer to conciliate.

USEFUL ADDRESSES

Advice Information and Mediation Services (AIMS)
Astral House
1268 London Road
London SW16 4ER
Tel: 020 8765 7465
Fax: 020 8765 7218
Email: aims@ace.org.uk
Run in association with Age Concern England, AIMS gives specialist advice and information on retirement housing, informs residents of their rights and helps resolve management problems. AIMS also offers a conciliation service to leaseholders and managers.

Association of Retirement Housing Managers (ARHM)
3rd Floor
89 Albert Embankment
London SE1 7TP
Tel: 020 7820 1839

Members manage most private retirement housing schemes in Britain. Their Code of Practice has been approved by Government and was introduced in 1996. Copies are available (price £10). Will look at complaints about members where not investigated by other bodies.

Centre for Sheltered Housing Studies
1st Floor
Elgar House
Shrub Bill Road
Worcester WR4 9EE
Tel: 01905 21155
Fax: 01905 22330

Committed to achieving high professional standards in retirement housing services, provides training for all categories of staff involved in providing services.

Elderly Accommodation Counsel
3rd Floor
89 Albert Embankment
London SE1 7TP
Tel: 020 7820 1343
Fax: 020 7820 3970
Email: enquiries@e-a-c.demon.co.uk

Maintains a nationwide database of all forms of accommodation for older people – sheltered housing for sale and rent, residential care homes, nursing homes and close care schemes. Staff also give guidance, advice and detailed information to help enquirers choose and fund the accommodation most suited to their needs.

Federation of Private Residents' Associations
3rd Floor
Overseas House
19–23 Ironmonger Row
London EC1V 3QN
Tel: 020 7490 7073

Advises leasehold residents' associations who are paid-up members on legal rights and management problems. Has an information pack on setting up a residents' association (price £10).

The Independent Housing Ombudsman
Norman House
105–109 Strand
London WC2R 0AA
Tel: 020 7836 3650
LoCall: 08457 125973

Investigates complaints about maladministration by registered social landlords. Any leaseholder who pays a housing association to manage or provide services can use this service.

Leasehold Advisory Service (LEASE)
8 Maddox Street
London W1R 9PN
Tel: 020 7493 3116

*Advice and information for leasehold owners of flats on enfranchise-
ment and legal rights.*

National Housing Federation
175 Gray's Inn Road
London WC1X 8UP
Tel: 020 7278 6571

*Campaigns on change in legislation, good practice, policy and devel-
opment, and other aspects of housing associations' activities. Produces
a range of publications; runs training courses and conferences.*

National House Building Council (NHBC)
Buildmark House
Chiltern Avenue
Amersham
Bucks HP6 5AP
Tel: 01494 434477

*Sets, regulates and improves house-building standards in the UK and
provides insurance protection for house buyers through its building
codes, including the Sheltered Housing Code.*

ABOUT AGE CONCERN

A Buyer's Guide to Retirement Housing is one of a wide range of publications produced by Age Concern England, the National Council on Ageing. Age Concern works on behalf of all older people and believes later life should be fulfilling and enjoyable. For too many this is impossible. As the leading charitable movement in the UK concerned with ageing and older people, Age Concern finds effective ways to change that situation.

Where possible, we enable older people to solve problems themselves, providing as much or as little support as they need. A network of local Age Concerns, supported by 250,000 volunteers, provides community-based services such as lunch clubs, day centres and home visiting.

Nationally, we take a lead role in campaigning, parliamentary work, policy analysis, research, specialist information and advice provision, and publishing. Innovative programmes promote healthier lifestyles and provide older people with opportunities to give the experience of a lifetime back to their communities.

Age Concern is dependent on donations, covenants and legacies.

Age Concern England
1268 London Road
London SW16 4ER
Tel: 020 8765 7200
Fax: 020 8765 7211

Age Concern Scotland
113 Rose Street
Edinburgh EH2 3DT
Tel: 0131 220 3345
Fax: 0131 220 2779

Age Concern Cymru
4th Floor
1 Cathedral Road
Cardiff CF1 9SD
Tel: 029 2037 1566
Fax: 029 2039 9562

Age Concern Northern Ireland
3 Lower Crescent
Belfast BT7 1NR
Tel: 028 9024 5729
Fax: 028 9023 5497

ABOUT ROOM (NATIONAL COUNCIL FOR HOUSING AND PLANNING)

Formed in 1999 from the merger between the National Housing and Town Planning Council (NHTPC, est. 1900) and the Housing Centre Trust, ROOM aims to improve the contribution of housing and planning to the social, physical and economic regeneration of local communities. Its strength is the breadth and diversity of its membership. Most local authorities are members, as are many housing associations, builders, private consultants, components manufacturers and individuals.

ROOM has 12 regions covering England and Wales. Each of the regions is active in local and regional matters. Further information about your region can be obtained from their Head Office, which will put you in touch with your Regional Secretary.

ROOM's key role is bringing together people across the many arbitrary professional and institutional boundaries which exist in housing and planning. It publishes *axis*, the Journal of Housing, Planning and Regeneration, six times a year.

ROOM (National Council for Housing and Planning)
14 Old Street
London EC1V 9BH
Tel: 020 7251 2363
Fax: 020 7608 2830
Email: mail@room.org.uk
Website: www.room.org.uk

PUBLICATIONS FROM AGE CONCERN BOOKS

Housing Options for Older People
Louise Russell

Although not everyone either wants or needs to move home just because they reach retirement age, some people will want to move and, for others, circumstances may arise which mean that they may have to move. This book aims to look at all the options open to older people (including staying put), and provides a realistic indication of how easy or difficult each option might be to pursue successfully. Topics covered include:

- whether to stay at home or move;
- living with relatives or friends;
- what type of housing is required;
- paying for repairs and improvements;
- options for people with limited capital;
- other options for home owners;
- buying or renting accommodation;
- raising income or capital from your home.

Written in straightforward language, this book will help readers to make well-informed decisions about their housing in retirement.

£6.99 0-86242-287-6

Your Taxes and Savings
Sally West and Money Management Council

Explains how the tax system affects older people over retirement age, including how to avoid paying more than necessary. The information about savings covers the wide range of investment opportunities now available.

For further information, please 0870 44 22 044

Your Rights: A guide to money benefits for older people

Sally West

Written in clear and concise language, *Your Rights* guides readers through the maze of benefits available and explains all of the main areas of interest to older people. The book contains up-to-date information on all key changes and provides specific sections on:

- retirement pensions;
- housing and council tax benefits;
- Income Support and the Social Fund;
- paying for residential care;
- help with legal and health costs.

For more information, please ring 0870 44 22 044

Using Your Home as Capital: A guide to raising cash from the value of your home

Cecil Hinton and David McGrath

Many older people own increasingly valuable homes but would like more income or capital to make the most of their retirement. This bestselling book, for home-owners in their 60s, 70s and 80s, gives a detailed explanation of how to safely capitalise on the value of your home and obtain a regular additional income.

Written in clear and straightforward language, *Using Your Home as Capital* provides all the information older people need when considering this complex area.

For more information, please ring 0870 44 22 044.

Better Health in Retirement

Dr Anne Roberts

A little attention to your body's changing needs and some knowledge of how to deal with common illnesses can lead to a long and healthy retirement. Written in non-medical language, Dr Anne Roberts gives practical, expert advice and information to help everyone keep as healthy as possible in later life. Topics include:

- developing a healthy lifestyle;
- health checks and screening;
- common illnesses of later life;
- using the health service;
- complementary medicines;
- help for older carers.

This book also provides clear guidance on areas such as depression, sleeping well and relaxation techniques. Positive and upbeat, this book will equip readers with all of the information needed to take charge of their own health.

£6.99 0-86242-251-5

If you would like to order any of these titles, please write to the address below, enclosing a cheque or money order for the appropriate amount made payable to Age Concern England. Credit card orders may be made on 0870 44 22 044 (for individuals); 0870 44 22 120 (AC federation, other organisations and institutions). Fax: 01626 323318.

Age Concern Books
PO Box 232
Newton Abbot
Devon TQ12 4XQ

AGE CONCERN INFORMATION LINE/FACTSHEETS SUBSCRIPTION

Age Concern produces 44 comprehensive factsheets designed to answer many of the questions older people (or those advising them) may have. Topics covered include money and benefits, health, community care, leisure and education, and housing. For up to five free factsheets, telephone: 0800 00 99 66 (7am–7pm, seven days a week, every day of the year). Alternatively you may prefer to write to Age Concern, FREEPOST (SWB 30375), ASHBURTON, Devon TQ13 7ZZ.

For professionals working with older people, the factsheets are available on an annual subscription service, which includes updates throughout the year. For further details and costs of the subscription, write to Age Concern at the above Freepost address.

INDEX